Contents

Discovering China

China is a land of opposites. It contains snow-capped mountains and scorching deserts. It has the highest point on the planet, and one of the lowest. Its culture has changed dramatically in only a few decades, yet its people still keep alive ancient traditions.

Many mouths to feed

With 1.3 billion inhabitants, China holds one-fifth of the population of the planet. In terms of area, China is the fourth-largest country in the world, after Russia, Canada and the USA.

People have lived in China for more than 4,000 years, making it one of the world's oldest civilisations. Until the twentieth century, much of China's development took place in isolation from the rest of the world.

▼ The People's Republic of China is made up of five autonomous regions, 22 provinces and four principalities.

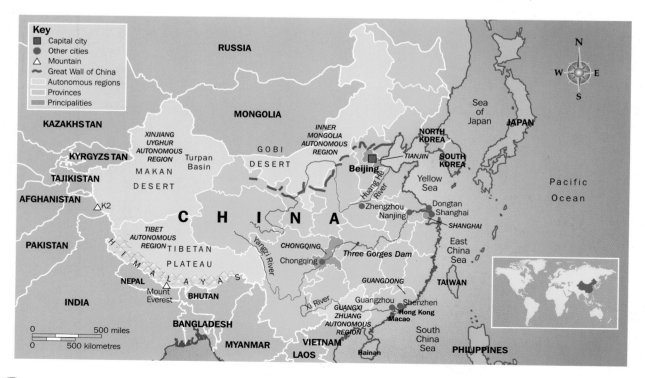

A century of change

For thousands of years, dynasties of emperors ruled China. That all changed in 1912 when China became a republic. In the same year, China's last emperor stepped down.

Throughout much of the first half of the twentieth century, China was torn apart by civil war and by conflict with Japan. In 1949, the Chinese Communist Party (CCP) took control of China. As leader of the CCP, Mao Zedong (1893-1976) became China's leader and the country was officially named The People's Republic of China.

Modern China

China remains a communist state. Under communism, the Chinese government controls all property and many aspects of people's daily life.

Following the death of Mao Zedong, the Chinese government began a major reform of the Chinese economy. State controls were lifted and the country's economy was opened up to foreign investment. As a result, China has been one of the world's fastest-growing nations for almost thirty years.

Today China has the world's fourth-biggest economy, after the USA, Japan and Germany. China's spectacular economic growth has meant that millions of its people have been lifted out of poverty.

China Statistics

Area: 9.6 million sq km (3.7 million sq miles)

Capital city: Beijing

Government type: Communist State

Bordering countries: Afghanistan, Bhutan, Burma, India, Kazakhstan, North Korea, Kyrgyzstan, Laos, Mongolia, Nepal, Pakistan, Russia, Tajikistan, Vietnam

Currency: Yuan (¥)

Language: Standard Chinese or Mandarin (Putonghua, based on the Beijing dialect), Yue (Cantonese), Wu (Shanghainese), Minbei (Fuzhou), Minnan (Hokkien-Taiwanese), Xiang, Gan, Hakka dialects, minority languages

▶ Beijing's spectacular 'Bird's Nest' stadium was the centrepiece of the 2008 Olympic Games.

Landscape and climate

China stretches for 5,500 km (3,400 miles) from north to south – about the same distance as from Sweden to the centre of Africa. It is no wonder that China has many different landscapes and climates.

Rivers

China has more than 50,000 rivers. The three main rivers are the Huang He, the Xi and the Yangzi. The Yangzi, the longest river in the country, rises in the Tibetan Highlands and flows across central China, draining into the East China Sea north of Shanghai.

In 2006 work was completed on a massive dam in the Three Gorges area of the Yangzi. The most important function of the Three Gorges Dam is to control flooding, which has often caused huge damage and loss of life throughout the area.

Facts at a glance

Land area: 9.3 million sq km (3.6 million sq miles)

Water area: 270,550 sq km (104,460 sq miles)

Highest point: Mount Everest 8,850 m (29,035 ft)

Lowest point: Turpan Pendi, −154 m (−502 ft)

Longest river: Yangzi River 6,300 km (3,915 miles)

Coastline: 14,500 km (9,010 miles)

⬇ The Three Gorges Dam on the River Yangzi is the world's largest hydro-electric power station.

DID YOU KNOW?
The huge Three Gorges Dam on the Yangzi River has created a reservoir about 600 km (373 miles) long – more than the distance between England and Germany.

Landscape regions

The landscape of China can be divided into three major regions: the south-west, the north-west and the east.

Mountains dominate south-west China. The north-west is largely desert. The east of China is generally low-lying, and most of the region is less than 450 m (1,500 ft) above sea level.

High and low

One-third of China's land area is mountainous. The Qingzang in south-west China is also known as the Tibetan Plateau. Most of this area is about 4,000 to 5,000 m (13,000-16,500 ft) above sea level. The vast plateau is surrounded by the Himalayan mountains, including the two highest peaks on Earth, Mount Everest and K2.

By contrast, one of the lowest points on Earth is the Turpan Basin in north-west China. The Turpan Basin covers an area of 50,000 sq km (20,000 sq miles). Like the Gobi and Taklamakan deserts, also in north-west China, this area is barren and very dry.

Climate

China's climate is as varied as its landscapes. The Tibetan Plateau has one of the harshest climates on Earth, with temperatures as low as −19 °C. In the north it can be extremely cold with sub-arctic temperatures in the winter months. Typhoons can occur in the south in the summer and winters are short. In the deserts of the north-west it is dry, hot and sunny in the summer and cold and dry in the winter.

◐ Himalayan peaks rise above the clouds in Chinese-occupied Tibet.

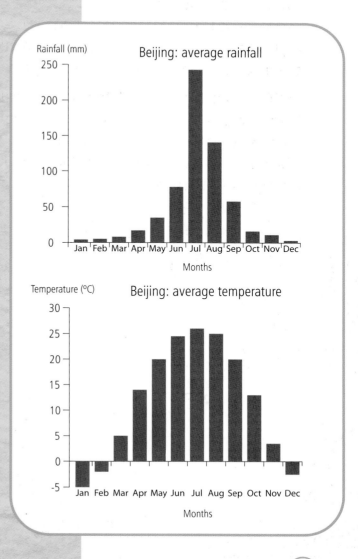

Rainfall (mm)

Beijing: average rainfall

Months

Temperature (°C)

Beijing: average temperature

Months

Population and health

China has more people than any country in the world and its population is growing by approximately 12-13 million each year. Han Chinese, who make up the vast majority of the population, are believed to be the largest single ethnic group in the world.

One-child policy

In the 1970s the Chinese government became alarmed by how fast the country's population was growing and decided to limit how many children people could have to one child per couple. Introduced in 1979, the 'one-child policy' applies to all couples living in cities, unless one or both partners are from an ethnic minority, or are themselves the only child of their parents.

The government claims that the one-child policy, has reduced the population by 400 million. Critics say it has led in some cases to the killing of baby girls because Chinese people prefer to have boys to continue the family line.

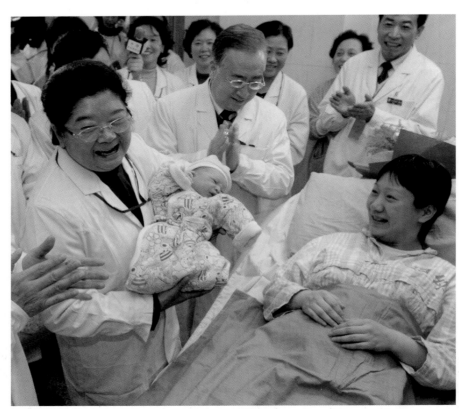

▶ At Beijing Maternity Hospital, staff congratulate a mother on the birth of China's 1.3 billionth citizen.

Life expectancy

As healthcare and living standards in China have improved, life expectancy has risen. In 1950, Chinese women lived on average to the age of 42 and men to the age of 39. Today women live on average to the age of 75 and men to the age of 71.

Health problems

Strokes, heart disease and cancer are the leading causes of death in China, but the country has a variety of other health problems. Many are caused by poor air and water quality in China's cities.

In such a densely populated country, diseases can spread quickly. In 2002 an epidemic of the potentially fatal Severe Acute Respiratory Syndrome (SARS) started in Guangdong Province, China. Within weeks the disease spread across China and to much of the world. The SARS outbreak was later stopped by countries working together to contain the virus.

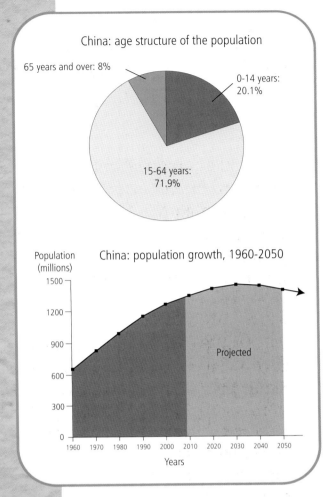

China: age structure of the population

65 years and over: 8%

0-14 years: 20.1%

15-64 years: 71.9%

China: population growth, 1960-2050

Population (millions)

Projected

Years

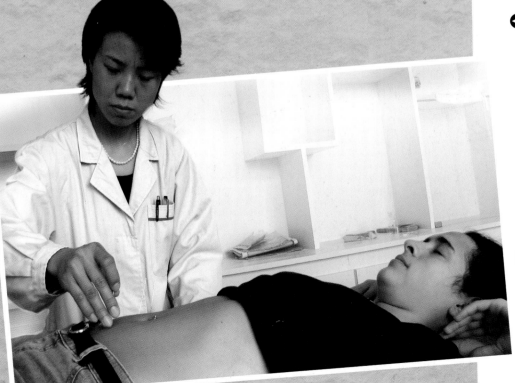

◀ A Chinese doctor treats a woman patient using acupuncture needles. The needles are inserted into special points on the body which are believed to control the flow of 'qi', a person's vital energy.

DID YOU KNOW? Traditional Chinese acupuncture dates back as far as the first millennium BCE. In modern China it is used to treat a range of ailments from migraines to rheumatism and back pain.

Settlements and living

With such a vast population, China faces a huge challenge to provide food and shelter for all its people. Most people live in rural areas, where poverty and hardship are common. About 12 million people move from rural to urban areas every year in search of a better life.

New cities

At present China is building a major new city each year to house its growing population. During the next 12 years, 20 new cities will need to be built each year as China struggles to provide homes for another 400 million people.

An important task will be to avoid the problems that already affect so many of China's urban areas: chronic overcrowding, traffic congestion and pollution.

▼ With its soaring high-rise buildings, Shanghai is the largest city in China as well as a major commercial and financial centre.

From village to super-city

One example of a new city is Shenzhen in southern China. From a small fishing village in the 1970s, it has grown into a major urban centre with a population of more than 8 million.

According to US Department of Commerce, in terms of industrial output, Shenzhen is the biggest manufacturing centre in the world. With a constant stream of new emigrants arriving from inland China, it is also one of the world's fastest-growing cities.

Dongtan eco-city

China is trying to look towards the future by developing environmentally-friendly cities with good air and water quality. Dongtan is one such eco-city being built in China.

Located on an island at the mouth of the Yangzi River, the city has been planned so that walking or cycling is quicker than driving. Giant windmills will provide energy for the city, which is planned to open in 2010.

City part-timers

Millions of Chinese people move to cities to find work but not all live there permanently. The capital, Beijing, for example, has China's second-largest population of 11.1 million, but at least 1 million of these people are students and migrant workers who go home during holiday periods.

Temporary residents are common in other cities in China. In Shanghai, the temporary population is 6.3 million people – in addition to its full-time population of nearly 19 million!

Facts at a glance

Urban population: 40.4% (530.6 million)

Rural population: 59.6% (782.3 million)

Population of largest city: 18.8 million (Shanghai)

▼ These traditionally built wooden houses are in a rural area of China's Guizhou Province.

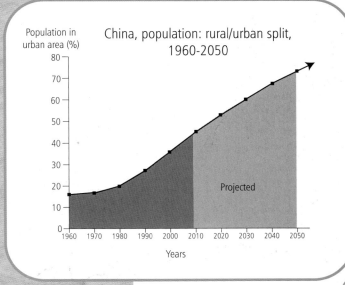

China, population: rural/urban split, 1960-2050

Population in urban area (%)

Projected

Years

Family life

Since the 1980s, family life in China has changed in many ways. As well as having fewer children, the Chinese are marrying and having children later in life. In the cities, more and more young people are also choosing to live together without getting married.

Changing values

Traditionally, Chinese people have always placed a high value on family relationships. In the past, a traditional household in China might include five generations and as many as 100 relatives, with the oldest male acting as overall head of the family.

Facts at a glance

Average children per childbearing woman:
1.8 children

Average household size:
3.6 people

▼ A Chinese couple and their baby son enjoy an afternoon out in a park in Beijing.

As a result of China's one-child policy, however, millions of Chinese people are now growing up without brothers and sisters. The divorce rate has also risen by almost 20 per cent, with 1.4 million couples filing for divorce in 2007.

Life at home

Chinese children live with their parents and sometimes with their grandparents too. Nearly everyone in China works until the retirement age, which is usually 60 for men and 55 for women. All Chinese people must stop work at the official retirement age.

In many households, grandparents look after the house and care for children during the day. Respect for older people is an important Chinese value, and children are taught to obey their elders from an early age.

Parents and grandparents

Chinese children have close relationships with their parents and grandparents. All Chinese citizens are required by law to care for their elderly parents. The family unit is usually led by the father, who strongly influences decisions of family members.

Children usually live with their parents until they are married. Some couples continue to live with their parents after they are married until they can afford a home of their own.

When children leave home they often prefer to live in the same neighbourhood as their parents.

This 100-year-old Chinese woman has spent the last 25 years of her life in a care home. Because of the one-child policy, China's old people have fewer family members to care for them, and many now depend on on state or private care.

Religion and beliefs

Since 1949, China has been an atheist country, and most forms of religion are officially discouraged. In Tibet, which China has occupied since 1959, it is against the law to practise the Tibetan form of Buddhism, but in China other forms of Buddhism, as well as Christianity and Islam, are practised quite openly.

Religion today

In China, two-fifths of the population claim to have no religious beliefs at all. However, a number of Chinese people (mostly non-Han Chinese) practise Buddhism or Islam and a growing minority of people in China are Christian.

Despite persecution by the occupying Chinese, most Tibetans still practise their traditional form of Buddhism. As more Han Chinese move into Tibet, Tibetans fear that

In Beijing's Lama Temple, Buddhist worshippers burn incense and pray for good luck on the first day of the Chinese New Year.

DID YOU KNOW?

Beijing's Lama Temple is one of the world's most ancient Buddhist shrines. Amongst many treasures, it contains an 18 m (60 ft) statue of the Buddha carved from a single piece of sandalwood.

their religion will die out. Tibet's spiritual leader is the Dalai Lama. He has lived in exile since 1959, travelling the world to tell people about the struggle of the Tibetan people.

Folk religions

Daoism and Confucianism are two belief systems that help guide many Chinese people. They are known as folk religions. About 29 per cent of Chinese people practise Chinese folk religions.

Daoism is over 4,000 years old. Its followers aim to find inner peace and harmony by living a simple life and not harming others. Confucianism is about 2,000 years old. It helps guide people on how to behave in society.

Festivals

More than 40 festivals are celebrated in China each year. Some celebrate national holidays such as New Year's Day, the Spring Festival, Youth Day and National Day. Others are local festivals. Many have their roots in ancient rituals in which people prayed for good crops or gave thanks for the harvest.

The Lantern Festival is a holiday that marks the end of the Chinese New Year. People hang colourful lanterns on their houses. There are parades and fireworks. This celebration dates back to 200 BCE.

⬤ The Dalai Lama, Tibet's spiritual leader, has spoken out strongly against the Chinese occupation of his homeland and the persecution of Tibetan Buddhists.

China: major religions

Traditional beliefs: 4.4%
Muslim: 1.5%
Non-religious: 39.2%
Atheist: 7.8%
Buddhist: 8.4%
Christian: 10%
Chinese folk religionist: 28.7%

▶ Dragons have been a symbol of health and good luck in China for 6,000 years. The dragon dance seen here is one of China's oldest and most colourful folk traditions.

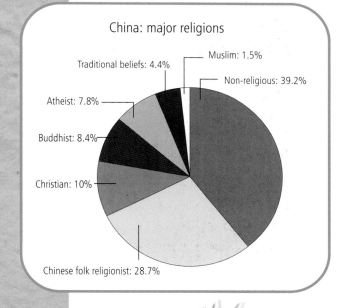

Education and learning

At the time of the founding of the People's Republic in 1949, 80 per cent of China's population were illiterate. Today, all citizens receive nine years' compulsory education and the country has a nationwide educational system with over 20 million students at college and university.

China's schools

The Chinese take education and learning very seriously. Schools in China are state-run, private or international. Classes in state-run schools can be large, with as many as 50 students, so those who can afford it often prefer to send their children to private or international schools.

Facts at a glance

Children in primary school:
Male 99%, Female 99%

Children in secondary school:
Male 74%, Female 75%

Literacy rate (over 15 years):
91%

▼ Primary school pupils in China work long hours, typically spending almost nine hours a day in the classroom.

Most Chinese children attend primary school for six years starting at the age of six or seven, then lower secondary school for three years. About two-thirds continue their education with three years of upper secondary school.

Subjects studied at school include Chinese, English, maths and sciences. Students also study Chinese literature and art. Many Chinese students start to learn English in primary school at the age of seven.

Higher education

Admission into university is highly selective and is based on exam results. Only one in ten students is accepted at a Chinese state university, so competition for places is fierce.

As well as six 'National Key Universities', which receive extra government support, China has 33 regional universities and hundreds of technical and other higher-learning colleges (about 1,000 altogether). State university education is paid for by the government. In return, university graduates must accept whatever job they are given by the Chinese government when they graduate. Typically students attend university for three or four years.

Private universities started about 20 years ago in China. Today there are about 1,300. They accept students who do not do well enough in their exams to go to a state university.

This Chinese character means 'long life'.

▶ Students and college leavers talk to potential employers at a job fair in southeast China's Fujian Province.

Employment and economy

For thousands of years China's economy was based on farming. That changed in the late 1970s when the communist government began the move to a free market economy. Since then, manufacturing and foreign trade have boomed – and China has become a very different place.

A growing economy

For the past 30 years, the Chinese economy has doubled in size every eight years. This huge growth has had a profound impact not only in China but all over the world.

China's new wealth is shared out very unevenly. In urban areas, economic growth is often twice as much as in rural areas. This has led to more rural workers leaving for the cities to find work, mostly in factories.

▼ High-rise office buildings dominate the skyline of Shanghai's financial district.

Facts at a glance

Contributions to GDP
  agriculture: 11.3%
  industry: 48.6%
  services: 40.1%
Labour force:
  agriculture: 43%
  industry: 25%
  services: 32%
Female labour force:
  44.1% of total
Unemployment rate: 4%

Jobs in China

As China's economy has grown, there have been losses as well as gains. For example, when the Chinese government turned state-owned industries over to the private sector, 27.8 million jobs were lost as businesses were modernised. Of the workers who were made redundant, only 18.5 million found jobs in other companies.

China has a massive labour force of more than 800 million people, but most live in rural areas where jobs are often scarce. In cities such as Shanghai, new high-tech businesses have grown up to replace traditional industries, but workers often lack the skills to fill the new jobs that have been created.

The challenge ahead

As demand falls and China struggles with the effects of the global recession, its economy faces huge problems. If the economy continues to grow, 8 million new jobs can be created each year. But each year 15 million new people enter the job market.

In 2009 the government announced ambitious plans to create jobs for 15 million Chinese workers. Despite this, unemployment in China is likely to be a big problem for the country for many years to come.

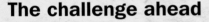 After a break for the Chinese New Year, migrant workers return from the countryside to find work in the city.

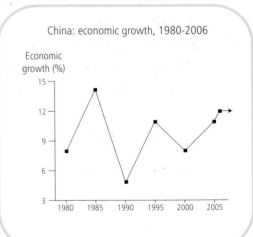

China: economic growth, 1980-2006

Economic growth (%)

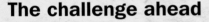 From 1980 to 2000, China's economic growth often dipped as the country made the transition to a market economy.

DID YOU KNOW? In China the economy has grown so fast that even the government cannot keep up with it. In 2006 it discovered that the economy was $100 bn bigger than it thought!

Industry and trade

In 2008 China exported more than $1.4 trillion worth of goods to over 230 countries around the globe, making it the world's second-largest exporter after the USA. However, like many other countries, China is facing a deepening recession and output is now falling sharply.

Natural resources

China has abundant natural resources. Minerals found in China include zinc, copper, lead, and iron ore. Many of China's industries are based on the processing of these resources. Factories produce iron, steel, fertilisers, textiles and cement.

▼ Large-scale industrial centres such as this steel plant in Beijing have generated huge wealth but have also scarred the landscape in many parts of China.

State control

To help encourage industry, the Chinese government controls prices of some minerals and other materials. The government also closely controls the use and supply of energy. Today many industries are still state-owned but this is changing as more and more businesses are sold to private investors.

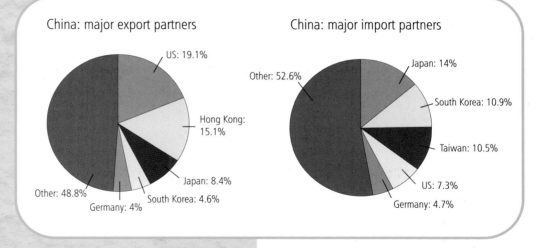

China: major export partners

- US: 19.1%
- Hong Kong: 15.1%
- Japan: 8.4%
- South Korea: 4.6%
- Germany: 4%
- Other: 48.8%

China: major import partners

- Japan: 14%
- South Korea: 10.9%
- Taiwan: 10.5%
- US: 7.3%
- Germany: 4.7%
- Other: 52.6%

Exports

China is known the world over for its consumer electronics, appliances, vehicles and paper products. Its main exports are machinery, electrical products, data processing equipment, clothing, textiles, steel and mobile phones.

But demand for goods has fallen as a result of the economic downturn. At least 70,000 factories in China have closed so far and many more are expected to fail in the coming years. Migrant workers have been especially hard hit, with over 10 million losing their jobs in 2008.

A changing world

In late 2008 China celebrated the thirtieth anniversary of its historic economic reforms. At the same time, demand for Chinese exports fell for the first time in years and unemployment rose to levels not seen in China since the 1980s.

China's government promised to continue reforming the economy. It called on the Chinese people to increase demand for Chinese products at home so China would be less dependent on exports in the future.

Many Chinese factory and industrial workers have lost their jobs as plants have closed because of the global recession.

21

Farming and food

Over the last 30 years farming in China has steadily declined. Today only 50 per cent of the workforce is employed on the land, compared to 70 per cent in 1979, and farming only accounts for about 11 per cent of China's output. Most of those who have left are now migrant labourers in China's cities.

Farming output

Despite the decline of farming, China's agricultural output is still the largest of any country in the world. As well as being the world's biggest rice grower, China produces wheat, potatoes, sorghum, peanuts, tea, millet, barley, cotton, oilseed, pork, and fish – all on a vast scale.

Facts at a glance

Farmland: 17% of total land area

Main agricultural exports: animal and vegetable materials prepared food

Main agricultural imports: soya beans, cotton, palm oil

Average daily calorie intake: 2,940 calories

🔻 Harvesting rice by hand is back-breaking, poorly-paid work. Covering their faces to protect against mosquitoes, labourers often have to work for hours up to their knees in muddy water.

Land use and ownership

Agricultural land in China is owned communally. Each village owns the land around it and local families hold a part of the land on a long-term lease.

Because arable land is scarce in China, every available plot is farmed, and intensive farming techniques are used to grow as much as possible.

At present huge areas of farmland are being swallowed up by China's growing cities. About 16 million acres of land (6.48 million hectares) has been lost to make way for urban projects in the last 20 years. In all, one-fifth of China's agricultural land has been lost since 1949.

DID YOU KNOW?

China's favourite drink is green tea or black tea – without milk or sugar. In fact, if you ask for white tea in China, you're likely to be offered a cup of steaming hot water!

⬥ Chinese tea shops sell many different varieties. Most are available only in China and are not exported.

Chinese food

For many years, China was badly affected by food shortages, and dairy products and meat were often in short supply. Today, the typical Chinese diet includes more protein, but the staple foods are still rice or noodles, and many people are vegetarians.

Chinese food is a balance of opposites – hot and cold, spicy and mild, fresh and preserved. Favourite Chinese dishes such as chicken chow mein and Peking duck are now enjoyed not just in China but all over the world.

▶ Instead of a knife and fork, Chinese food is eaten with chopsticks. The tapering sticks are manoeuvered in one hand, between the thumb and fingers, and used to pick up bite-size portions of food.

Transport and communications

China's transport system has expanded rapidly since the 1980s. However, the country still lacks an efficient, nationwide transport network, and in some areas steam locomotives are still used to transport supplies such as coal to industrial centres.

Distance travel

Rail is the most common form of transport for goods and for people travelling long distances. China's rail network covers the entire country and is the third-biggest in the world. Like all China's transport systems, it is concentrated mainly in coastal areas and along major rivers.

Facts at a glance

Total roads: 1.9 million km (1.1 million miles)
Paved roads: 1.6 million km (979,014 miles)
Railways: 75,438 km (46,875 miles)
Major airports: 47
Major ports: 8

▼ Shanghai's rail network is the first commercial high-speed 'maglev' line in the world. Cushioned by magnetic forces, the trains can reach speeds of up to 501 kph (311 mph).

Getting around

Rural areas are often remote from the main transport networks, so country-dwellers depend on traditional ways of getting around, such as cycling or walking.

China has been working to improve its road network since the 1950s, but around 400,000 km (250,000 miles) of it are still unsurfaced. China's roads support nearly 160 million motor vehicles.

On your bike

There are about half a billion bicycles in China – more than in any other country – and bicycles outnumber cars on the road by ten to one. Sometimes the sheer number of bicycles even causes traffic jams. As more people have started driving cars in China, the number of road accidents has increased, many of them caused by Chinese cyclists riding against the flow of the traffic.

Travel by boat

On China's waterways many different types of boat are used to transport goods and people. Barges carry raw materials to factories and manufactured goods to ports. Sampans are a type of houseboat commonly found in southern China. Fishermen live with their families on these boats.

Modern communications

As well as the rapid spread of Internet use and mobile phones (see panel), broadcasting has also developed quickly in the new China. China Central Television is the major state television broadcaster and is watched by more than one billion viewers.

△ Cyclists stream past the Gate of Heavenly Peace in Beijing's Tiananmen Square.

DID YOU KNOW?
The Chinese junk is one of the most successful types of sailing ship in history. First developed in 220 BCE, junks could carry up to 700 passengers and were often used for long sea voyages.

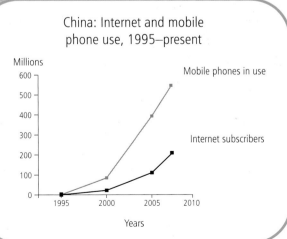

China: Internet and mobile phone use, 1995–present

Millions

Mobile phones in use

Internet subscribers

Years

Leisure and tourism

With the steady rise in living standards over the past 30 years, Chinese people are now able to choose from a growing range of different ways to spend their leisure time.

Keeping fit

Physical exercise is a regular part of the lives of about 40 per cent of Chinese people. They exercise three times per week for at least half an hour at a time.

Favourite ways to keep fit in China include walking and jogging, followed by table tennis, badminton and tennis. Basketball is also popular among young people in the cities.

Martial arts

China is known for its martial arts which have the longest history of any sport and are still practised by millions of Chinese. People who regularly perform martial arts such as tai chi believe that it improves their vital energy, or 'qi'.

▶ Tai chi is a popular form of exercise in China and is widely practised for its health benefits.

Facts at a glance

Tourist arrivals (millions)

1995	20.0
2000	31.2
2005	46.8
2006	50.0
2007	131.8

▶ Chinese men enjoy a game of mahjongg in a tea house in southern China.

△ Mahjongg tiles marked with Chinese characters

Film and entertainment

When China opened up its economy in the late 1970s, it also opened up its film industry. As of 2009, China was the world's fifth-biggest producer of feature-length films. Since 2001 the government has limited the number of foreign films shown in China to 20 each year to encourage people to watch Chinese-made films.

Television is also popular in China, but is carefully monitored by the government, which often 'blacks out' news reports by foreign networks. Recent blacked-out content has included items about unrest in Tibet and negative coverage of the 2008 Beijing Olympics.

Tourism

China is the world's fourth-largest country for inbound tourism, and its revenue from tourism is growing by about 10 per cent each year. Tourists flock to sites such as the Great Wall of China, the Terracotta Army and the Forbidden City in Beijing.

According to the World Tourism Organisation, China will become the world's biggest tourist destination by 2020.

△ Created by China's first emperor for protection in the next life, the Terracotta Army has attracted millions of visitors from all over the world since it was first discovered in 1974.

Environment and wildlife

As China's population and economy have grown, its environment has suffered. All ten of the world's most polluted cities are in China, and in many areas the damage caused to the landscape by heavy industry will take decades to repair.

China's endangered wildlife

China is home to thousands of species of animals and plants. It has more than 3,800 species of fish and hundreds of amphibians that live in its rivers, lakes and coastal areas. Because their habitat is being steadily destroyed, many of these species are now under threat.

▼ Before the building of the Three Gorges Dam, the Yangzi river contained countless fish and animal species, including the now-extinct Chinese river dolphin.

The Chinese government has created over 1,200 reserves to protect rare animal and plants. But this is very unlikely to remove the threat to China's wildlife.

Expanding cities

As cities expand, China's wildlife habitats are shrinking. Forests are under threat due to logging and clearing of the land for farming. Deserts in western China are expanding by more than 6,700 sq km (2,587 sq miles) every year because of tree-cutting and overgrazing.

Meanwhile, coal dust, factory fumes, vehicle exhaust and wind-blown desert sand make Chinese cities some of the most polluted on Earth. Many of the country's rivers are polluted, and water in urban areas is heavily contaminated.

Carbon emissions

The growth of China's cities and factories has taken a huge toll on the environment. On the verge of being the world's largest energy consumer, China has overtaken the US as the world's largest emitter of carbon dioxide.

The vast country consumes more coal than the US, EU and Japan combined. The burning of coal is particularly bad for the environment as it creates climate-changing gases and causes acid rain.

The future

China is participating in talks on climate change, has banned all plastic bags, and spends more than $200 billion each year (10 per cent of GDP) on its pollution problems. Even so, many critics complain that this is not nearly enough to tackle China's problems.

DID YOU KNOW? A World Bank survey has claimed that about 460,000 Chinese people die prematurely each year as a result of breathing polluted air and drinking dirty water.

▼ The giant panda is native to the mountain regions of south-west China. Because of the destruction of their habitat and over-hunting, only about 1,600 now remain.

Glossary

amphibian animals that can live on land and in water

atheist person who does not believe in God

Buddhism major religion in Asia

Christian person who believes in Jesus Christ and his teachings

civilisation developed society that has political and social groups as well as arts and sciences

civil war war fought by different groups in the same country

climate normal weather conditions of an area

communism system in which all people are meant to have an equal share of a nation's property and wealth

Confucianism belief system based on the teachings of Confucius (551-479 BCE)

contagious easily spread from one person to another

culture way of life and traditions of a particular group of people

Daoism belief system based on balancing of opposites

developing country a country with a high level of poverty and low income and education levels

dynasty a ruling family

ecology the plants, animals and other organisms that share a habitat

economy way that trade and money are controlled by a country

endangered in danger of becoming extinct

export good or service that is sold to another country

extended family family that includes parents, grand-parents and other close relatives

extinct no longer living

free market economy in which the price of goods and services is fixed by laws of supply and demand

GDP total value of goods and services produced by a country

import good or service that is bought from another country

industry activity that processes or manufactures raw materials into finished products

Islam religion practised by Muslims

landscapes physical features of a place, such as mountains, rivers and deserts

manufacturing making products, usually from raw materials

natural resources water, soil, trees and minerals that are found naturally in an area

pollution substances that contaminate or poison, such as chemical waste

private owned by people rather than the government

raw material an ingredient that is used to produce something else; trees are the raw material used to make paper

reform change a system so it works better

republic a system of government in which people elect officials to make decisions on their behalf

reserve an area of land that is set aside to protect the habitat, wildlife or people living there

reservoir human-made or natural lake used for storing water

rural to do with the countryside or agriculture

species group of animals or plants that share common features

textile fabric such as cotton

typhoon a tropical storm

unemployment being without paid work

urban to do with cities and city life

Topic web

Use this topic web to explore Chinese themes in different areas of your curriculum.

Geography
Look at a map and visualise how many countries in Europe can fit into China. Make a list of all the countries that could fit.

Science
Find out more about acid rain. What are its causes and how does it affect the environment?

History
For decades, China was caught up in civil war. Find out who fought in the war and what each side wanted. How was the fighting finally brought to an end?

Maths
More than 400 million people in China work in agriculture. If the world population is 6.8 billion, what percentage of the world population works on a farm in China?

China

English
Write a letter to a student in China describing how your school day is different from theirs.

Citizenship
Do you think China's one-child policy is fair? Do you think a policy like that would work in the UK? Why, or why not?

Design and Technology
Imagine building a new city for millions of residents. What are the five most important things you would consider when building it?

ICT
Search online to find out about more about the Chinese calendar. Which animal represents the year in which you were born?

Further information and index

Further reading

China (Eyewitness Books), Hugh Sebag-Montefiore (Dorling Kindersley, 2007)
China (Looking at Countries), Jillian Powell (Franklin Watts, 2006)
China (The Changing Face of), Stephen Keeler (Wayland 2007)

Web

http://kids.nationalgeographic.com/Places/Find/China
This site contains facts and information on Chinese places and culture.
http://news.bbc.co.uk/1/hi/world/asia-pacific/country_profiles/1287798.stm
This is the BBC news page for China with links to recent events and background information.

Index

First published in 2010 by Wayland
Copyright Wayland 2010

This paperback edition first published by Wayland in 2011.

Wayland
Hachette Children's Books
338 Euston Road
London NW1 3BH

Wayland Australia
Level 17/207 Kent Street,
Sydney, NSW 2000

Editor: Paul Manning
Designer: Paul Manning
Consultants: Rob Bowden and Professor Morris Rossabi,
Distinguished Professor, City University of New York

Produced for Wayland by
White-Thomson Publishing Ltd

www.wtpub.co.uk
+44 (0)845 362 8240

British Library Cataloguing in Publication Data

Crean, Susan.
China. (Discover Countries)
1. China Juvenile literature.
I. Title II. Series
951'.06-dc22

ISBN-13: 9780750266925

Printed in Malaysia
Wayland is a division of Hachette Children's Books
an Hachette UK company
www.hachette.co.uk

All data in this book was researched in late 2009
and has been collected from the latest sources available at that time.

Picture credits

Cover l, Shutterstock/Lijuan Guo; r, Shutterstock/Sergei Bachlakov; 1, 15b, Shutterstock/Sergei Bachlakov; 3t, Shutterstock/Kriangsak; 3b, Shutterstock/Cora Reed; 4 (map), Stefan Chabluk; 5t, Shutterstock/Adam.golabek; 5b, Corbis/Gao Xueyu; 6, Corbis/Du Huaju; 7, Corbis/Jeremy Horner; 8, Corbis/Xinhua Press/XinHua; 9, Shutterstock/Luisa Fernanda Gonzalez; 10, Shutterstock/Claudio Zaccherini; 11, Shutterstock/Mujun; 12, Corbis/Xinhua Press/XinHua; 13, Corbis/Ryan Pyle; 14, Corbis/Diego Azubel; 15t, Shutterstock/Falk Kienas; 16, Corbis/Gideon Mendel; 17t, Shutterstock/Princess Lola; 17, Corbis/Zhang Guojun; 18, Shutterstock/Claudio Zaccherini; 19, Corbis/EPA/Mark; 20, Corbis/Ryan Pyle; 21, Shutterstock/Zhuda; 22, Shutterstock/Gautier Willaume; 23a, Corbis/Atlantide Phototravel; 23b, Shutterstock/Pablo H. Caridad; 24, Shutterstock/Lee Prince; 25, Photoshot; 26, Corbis/EPA/Michael Reynolds; 27t, Shutterstock/Yanfei Sun; 27m, Shutterstock/Frank Anusewicz; 27b, Shutterstock; 28, Shutterstock; 29a, Shutterstock/Kldy.

discover countries

China

Susan Crean

WAYLAND